DIVINE WILL

AF428633

Geetha Ramesh

ISBN 979-8-89363-969-8

THIS BOOK IS DEDICATED TO MY GRANDFATHER J RAMASAMI
WHO LIVED A SPIRITUAL LIFE AND SAW DIVINITY IN ALL BEINGS

Contents

Introduction

My humble salutations to the fellow souls of this human race. This Book is a dedication in love and service to the whole mankind.

Ever since my childhood I have been pondering over the existence of the world who might have created it and what is all that which keeps happening day and night.

Even before I could contemplate on whatever is happening around me I was pulled into the whirlpool of worldly existence.

Little did I know then that the life we are leading is already pre-designed for everything and anything we do. An Internal force from inside us is already governing us.

I have already lived sixty years of my life in this world. Whatever knowledge or experience I have gained I would like to share it with you all.

Life is not the same as how it used to be fifty years ago. Science and technology have improved on one side while on the other side increase in violence and crime has raised. Morality has come down. Selfishness has replaced sacrifice and selflessness.

Though we talk about globalization in all fields, the real globalization is the unity of minds. We need more of real love. Love for humanity, generosity, tolerance, patience and compassion.

The basic thing that mankind requires is conquer of self. The moment you have conquered your own self; you are the master of your own self. No force on earth can ever dare to shake you.

This conquest of self has to be taught early in one's life. This is the main foundation on any individual's life.

Self again can be divided into two, the physical level and the mental level. The gross level and the subtle level. There is something called the higher self or the divine self which governs us.

Physical level is divided into physical growth and health. Mental level consists of three parts super consciousness, sub consciousness and consciousness. Whether it is at the physical or mental level everything depends upon the input it gets. Thought is the main seed in anyone's life that is the foundation stone of our life. Our destiny or karma is based on thoughts. Like mind, body also has memories. Just like our body keeps on changing from birth to death, our mind also will not be the same throughout our life. It keeps on changing. As it changes so does our attitude, behaviour, habits, character and personality.

But there is something called foundation, which holds more good for the body than for the mind. The input for the body is the food that the mother eats during her pregnancy. Hence the role of the mother is very important. As she lays the foundation stone of an individual not only physically but also for his mental structure.

Just like our body is formed based on our genes, heredity and the intake of food, exercises and relaxation that we give to it, our mind is also formed based on our genes and the input that we give to it, going one step ahead mind also has memories from its previous births.

Our higher self is nothing but our soul which is divine in nature. It is the soul, which chooses its mother before entering the womb. While choosing the womb, it is also choosing its own destiny, the consequences of being born in that womb.

That is why a woman is definitely more important in her role as a mother. She is a form of energy (Shakti). Women can bear anything. They are the powerhouse of tolerance and patience. She is like a candle illuminating the world with her love. Women burn their energy in bringing up children and family.

All creatures on this earth are a composition of both qualities of positivity and negativity. They are two different sides of the same coin.

Let us move on to the actual book where more focus is laid on stability of mind and self-control. Before moving to control of mind and stability in all situations, thought process has to be closely observed.

Most of the Ideas of this book are based on teachings of Swami Vivekananda and Bhagwat Gita. These are all doctrines of Hindu religion, carried forward since ages. I have tried my level best to highlight on all these doctrines, for the sake of youngsters of this **era**.

To quote our great Indian spiritual master Swami Vivekananda "It may be that I shall find it good to get outside of my body, to cast it off like a disused garment. But I shall not cease to work! I shall inspire men everywhere until the world should know that it is one with God."

I feel responsible and find it my duty to share my knowledge from that great spiritual giant Swami Vivekananda. He has kept a vast treasure of knowledge distributed among his various volumes. I have tried my level best to bring out that knowledge in a nutshell for the common man to understand.

Chapter1
THOUGHT PROCESS

*Photo taken by author

Majority of us are under the impression that mind is inside the body. Actually it is the other way round. Body is inside the mind. Like breath, like air, like light, like God, we cannot see the mind. Everything great and wonderful is kept as a mystery unseen but more powerful. That is the wonderful game of the supernatural.

Our human system is also like computer, the input that we give to the system are like the programs of a computer. Inputs mainly as food focuses not only on the development of the body but for the mind as well. Mind takes input from various sources through the senses. Suppose a person is devoid of all the senses. He is blind, dumb and deaf. Will his mind work? Yes, his mind still works. Like body everybody has a mind also. We are one step greater than the animals due to our mind and thoughts. It is thoughts which makes human beings more powerful. Thoughts maketh a man. You become what you think All the inputs that we receive through our senses finally settle down as thoughts and impressions in our mind.

Our mind is the storage of millions and millions of such impressions recorded over the ages. In Hindu religion these impressions are the basis of karma. Our destiny itself is decided by these impressions which include our birth and death as well.

Each second we keep on spurning lots and lots of thoughts recording and rerecording. The process goes on. Physically we are all small islands of flesh and blood. Though the constituents are the same to everyone. At the mental plane also we are all small bubbles bundled with our thought impressions. But all the bubbles are part of the same ocean. We are all parts of one Huge Universal Mass.

Though gene and the inputs we receive as impressions when we are in the womb are partly responsible for our character, our childhood, the people around us, the incidents which we come across., the inputs received through our senses, all that which we come across from infancy to youth are the major foundation for the thought process.

Till youth the thoughts grow as tree, in middle age it gives us lot of experiences to cud chew during old age.

Let us not be a Pebble in the flowing river, let us become the roaring wave itself which emerges in the ocean.

*Photo taken by author

During our life span we come across several kinds of persons around us. The important characters in our life are very often repetitions from several births. Hence relationship with people is pivotal in shaping our destiny. In fact, our whole life depends upon this. No man is an island. Though physically and mentally we are separate, we are all part of one huge Universal Mass.

The sum total thoughts of a group of individuals is very important. It has moved Nations. It has created history. It has brought out many evolutions and revolutions. World War One and two and epidemics are examples of such mass up surging. That is at the macro level.

Even at the micro level mass thinking and reacting pushes a person to a wrong route which he chooses. For example, a group of individuals, mostly family members think that so and so is useless, so and so is lazy, so and so is vagabond and so and so is intelligent, beautiful etc. We can add on many such phrases, which only leads the individual to a false image of himself.

Some are born with excellent talents, intelligence and even with good character and a loving heart, but ironically their bad habits and mannerisms most of the time ruin their life itself. Some may be dull and less more obedient and disciplined, but their life will come out excellently well. Very often they may be children born from the same womb and brought up by same parents, where lies the difference.

Have you ever wondered why some people commit crimes? Crimes of various sort like murder, rape, bomb blast and terrorism. While some are more prone to suicide. Many have gone either mad or Psychos. Root cause of everything begins from childhood itself. Society, parents, teachers, friends, family members, neighborhood, their ancestors in the form of genes are to be blamed. Probe into the history of any individual everything traces back to his childhood.

One might have come across several kinds of persons around them, the positive ones, the negative ones, the neutral ones, the round character, that is, people having all emotions and attitudes, mixture of everything and the flat character (either positive or negative side of them is highlighted.)

But all Souls whether he is a positive person or a negative character have their inbound divinity within them. Basically, all Souls are divine, and they are rays from one Universal Master.

Souls cannot be destroyed. In fact, they cannot be seen also. Beauty of the Universal Soul can be seen everywhere. Universal soul when fragmented as individuals pass through a very long journey taking several births. In each birth the consciousness gathers certain memories carrying it forward. The purpose of our existence here on this earth is to learn. To learn through our experiences in each birth until finally the individual soul merges with the Universal soul. The main stage for this universal learning is mind and its thoughts.

Emotions upsurge as fountains from thoughts. Now emotions, like thoughts, are various in colors. Frequent thinking of the same thought gives power and energy to the thought. This holds good for all kinds of emotions.

Especially in love, this is very obvious. Two individuals, may be miles apart, but the communication between the two souls happens like lightning. Similarly, in hatred. One emotion spreads from one individual to the other. All emotions whether negative or positive have their own power and vibration.

At times a positive emotion like love can bring out negative thinking like fear, jealousy, possessiveness and attachment. Parents have too much love for their children that it brings out fear in them. Very often than not, have you noticed mothers worrying about their children with the negative fears? Fathers thinking negative about their son's future. These unnecessary thoughts and fears ruined the life of many an individual. Whenever a person is very serious with sickness, majority of them will have negative thoughts of fear of death.

Always think positive. Extend your positivity to the maximum if you really want to help the other individual. Think positive about your children. It will definitely boost their personality and morale. Positive thoughts towards a sick person will cure him and lead to recovery.

No doubt the pen is mightier than the sword, but still mightier is the mind and its thoughts. Sometimes the mind becomes so cruel, that for love for one's caste or status, people kill their own children.

*Photo taken by author

Chapter 2
Self-control

In this chapter, we will see how emotions rise from thoughts. A single thought may enter our mind as tiny as a mustard. Eventually, depending upon the situations around us, it will involve us like a mountain or a volcano. A good thought is always welcome and a boon. A negative thought when not checked and controlled properly by any individual will ruin his own life. That is why we see so many murders, suicides, rapes, bomb blasts, violence and whatnot.

Do you think that the individuals or groups who pursue that negative action are unaware of its consequences? In many cases at the depth of their heart they are more good and broad minded than a typical good person.

Knowingly or unknowingly they have sown the seed of negativity in their minds due to situation, persons and circumstances. They are caught in their own spider web from which they find it difficult to come out.

Many of the crimes, especially suicides, didn't happen suddenly on one fine day. Those were the cactus and weeds of negativities deposited in their minds over the years.

Negativity at its base level is just a gossip tearing apart another individual's life story with full gusto and enjoyment by group of individuals. At the macro level, which is the War itself.

I personally feel that the frequent outbreak of pandemics like swine flu, Corona, etc. are the sum total negative impressions gathered by individual minds over the years. In the past it used to burst as War like World War 1 and 2.

What do you think is basically the root cause of wars? At the base level it is greed, jealousy, selfishness, hatred and fear.

Even animals do not steep down to the level as humans do. We must develop the art of controlling our own self. Nowadays, women have also increased in criminal activities like murder, kidnapping etc. Of late there was a news of Karnataka woman murdering her own 4-year-old son so that he doesn't meet his father. This is the height of jealousy and selfishness.

Just because many are criminals does not mean that others are Saints. All Souls have to pass through several stages before they get finally enlightened and merged with universal consciousness. It is like how a river passes through several mountains and pits before it merges into the ocean. The physical body passes through several stages from infancy to old age. In its physical growth, the mind and the individual consciousness passes through a long journey. It is the turn of every individual soul to pass through various characters, not only in one birth, But in several births. We are like actors playing on the stage. So nothing is permanent in the worlds stage. A poor man may be rich in his next birth. A beggar might have been a millionaire in his previous birth, a beautiful woman might have been an ugly duckling two births ago. A criminal or even a rapist might have been a Saint in his previous birth. Nothing is permanent

Once the above truth gets grounded in everybody's mind, many of the problems could be solved. Even massive problems at the national and international level can be solved.

Self-control at the individual level cannot be attained unless we register the universal truth at our subconscious level.

There are only a few things to remember.

Death is certain. All who are born have to die. While death is certain, time of our death is not certain. There is no ownership to anybody. Whatever we possess as wealth, health, status, caste, education is all temporary and vanishes the moment you die. Only Death is truth. Rest is all stage play. There is no good, bad, positive and negative, happiness and sorrow, profit and loss, heat and cold. They are all changing patterns which everyone has to experience here on earth. We have come here to learn, let us die with knowledge.

Best knowledge is learning about our own self. A king might have conquered several kingdoms, but he is not a true warrior if he has not conquered his own self. Control of self lies not only in balancing your thoughts and emotions, but also in the ability to overcome natural tendencies. Each time you come out successfully from any given emotion, you become stronger. Think it was test of your willpower by Providence. When thoughts are like seeds, emotions and feelings are like hidden plants which will sprout in any suitable situation. Victoriously facing these situations with balanced thought and emotion without much turmoil or damage makes your Will strengthened. More strengthened Wills and strong men makes a better society and nation.

That does not mean that the World should be full of roses and no thorns. All roses have to be with thorns. What will life be without difficulties or negativities? It will be a complete boredom, like a movie without a villain.

Basically the following are the major negative emotions that generate in any individual. Fear, Ego, desire, jealousy, selfishness, hatred, lust, greed, anger, laziness, intolerance, impatience, impulsiveness, doubt, and fanaticism. Fear is one inborn quality in all living things. It is instinctive and instant in nature. Except fanaticism and ego, all the above given feelings are common in both man and animal. Where lies the difference. All the above emotions will be there in all individuals. The way you overcome the feeling according to the situation brings harmony and balance to your life. The more you get exposed to people and situations, the more you get entangled with any of the above negative emotions. Like a warrior, you have to take everything as a challenge.

Let us discuss about our major enemy, fear. Even though fear is common with animals, they have only one fear, that is death. But mankind has a very big list of fears death, disease, marriage, divorce, job, people, fear of losing someone or something, insult, fear of loss, hatred linked fear of cats, dogs, snakes, lizards, cockroaches, fear of failure, darkness, black magic, enemies, robbers, terrorism, etcetera.

Fear of death and disease, are natural and not in our hands. But the other kinds of fear can be eliminated. The more you eliminate such fears, the more confident you become. Fear is the greatest challenge we can face. For example, if someone has stage fear, he can deliberately appear on stages and perform. The more he does, his fear gets eliminated.

Similar exercises we can do for other emotions as well. Running away from any problem is not the solution. Nature will make you face the problem until and unless you get relieved from that particular emotion. That doesn't mean that one should get exposed to tigers and snakes. We should keep our mindset, always ready to face anything, and never to panic. To learn the lesson of self-control is very important in life. Certain incidents and same kind of people keep repeating in our life, as our thoughts have been energized by frequently thinking in one direction. We are not mature enough to come out of similar situations victoriously. It may take even one whole life time to learn it.

Ego is thinking too high of oneself. All creatures, especially human beings are equal on this earth. We are made of the same composition. Thinking too much of oneself is only foolishness. In this birth, someone may be a beggar. He might become a king in his next birth, and a negro may be born as a white in his next birth. A criminal may be a Saint in his next birth. A Brahmin might have been a Shudra in his previous birth. A beautiful woman might have been an ugly duckling in her previous birth, everything is temporary and time bound. There is nothing to be proud of. Whatever we achieve, also is possible only if nature gives us the blessing.

Now talking about desire, desire for mankind is very vast like an ocean. There is no limit to it. Like thoughts, desire keeps changing at each age and sometimes from month to month, person to person. As far as desire is concerned, it is better, we analyse and observe yourself. Desires which are not harmful to others and to self can be fulfilled.

In your eagerness to change yourself and to control yourself don't you ever suppress yourself of your natural urges, thoughts and behavior. Suppression only leads to aggressiveness. Any natural flow of thought or emotion just allow it to flow.

You are not an island of thought patterns. You are always a part of communal thought flow. The general thought patterns in and around you will definitely have its impact on you. It's like the common weather. Have you ever noticed in the classroom or in an office room when one person is gloomy he spreads the feeling to the whole room? When there is laughter, the whole place is filled with happiness.

Now coming back to desire. If any desire is unchecked, it becomes an addiction. It is desire for coffee or liquor that makes a person coffee addict or a drunkard. Addiction very often kills the person itself. Once we become a victim of some habit, it is very difficult to come out. We have to sit and analyze and council our self before we make a resolution to eliminate the habit. Even then, it may take years to eradicate that habit. One method is to reduce step by step. Suppose we take 6 coffees a day. We can gradually bring it down from 5,4,3,2.

And when you bring it down to one coffee, it may take even more time to eradicate. Unless you warn yourself of the consequences, it will create on your health, it is difficult to stop this final coffee. or there is another method of substituting coffee with some health drink or soup etc.

Waking up late in the morning or resolutions to do exercises and meditations are the common drawbacks people generally face. Only if you make a strong goal you can come out of these drawbacks.

To eliminate other negative emotions except fanaticism, we have to deliberately test ourselves by creating such situations where we get jealousy, hatred, selfishness etc. But before that we have to prepare ourself mentally. And by strengthening our will, we can come out of these situations victoriously. We must learn to be more selfless. Selflessness is a very high and noble quality which not only broadens our mind and strengthens our will, but also makes us universal. By becoming selfless and by sacrifices, we come more close to nature, to the creation itself. We become universal in nature.

Today, more and more of universal love and universal responsibility is required. People have failed to remember the universal truth that we are all different components of the same universe, both at the gross and subtle level, at both the physical and mental level. Unless we remember this consciously, we cannot bring it to practice in our routine. Conscious and regular practice is required.

People of late have become more fanatic and controversial. There are groups and clans within a nation, within a religion, within a state, within a party, within a caste, etcetera. If you take any small entity or 4 or 5 people, you will find two groups in that. Fanaticism is an extended form of ego. Eradicating fanaticism at its base level is much better for all nations.

Even if we are at equilibrium throughout the day when an advanced situation arises we react according to the emotions stored in our sub consciousness. In the next chapter let us discuss about the stability of mind.

*Photo taken by author

Chapter 3
Stability of Mind

*Photo taken by author

When we talk of stability of mind we should not forget to remember one biological reason that is secretion of hormones. Hormones play a major part in our behavioral pattern. Our thought pattern may be based on our internal and external knowledge, but behaviour depends mainly on biological factors.

A person may be very good at heart, well brought up and self-controlled basically, but if there is a disturbance within his body due to hormonal changes or health issues he is very likely to become frustrated and provoked with anger. He may burst out with anger and become short tempered. Sometimes people get aggravated due to extreme summer and lazy due to winter.

Especially with women there is a symptom called premenstrual tension. Due to chemical changes in the body, the women tends to become aggressive, quarrelsome, sometimes violent, and even lustful.

If stability of mind is achieved, most of the divorces can be reduced. Stability of mind is different from self-control. Stability of mind is how we react to any given situation. The inner change in any human being can be brought only when his beliefs, opinions, attitudes and his inner storage of information is widely changed. Change in internal storage of information is not a possibility as it was a process which took place right from his infancy. With added information, only the beliefs, opinions and attitudes can be changed. The world is like a forest, full of thorns, wild animals and other natural calamities. You cannot change the world, if you want to be protected, you have to be precautious. But leading a comfortable and secular life is not going to serve the purpose. Being 100% puritan is like a wall or wood. Life is experimental here on earth. You have come to experience the various colors and dramas of life. It is better to make a mistake and learn in due course of our action than to sit still like a stone with neither action nor emotion. Hence your experience in this world and how you face the situations and people in your life is more important. Your mind is the main playground or stage where everything is enacted. We may feel that so many things are happening at the physical level or in the exterior world, but the actual drama or Game is going on in the inner mind. Mind is a stage which receives all impressions and commands the body to act accordingly.

At the end of your life you will realize everything moved so fast like a dream, creating only memories. Very often than not people who commit mistakes or sins are not innocent or ignorant people, they are the very intelligent and knowledgeable ones. There is no use repenting at the end of your life.

Self-observation and introspection is very important if we want to achieve stability in our mind. Be observant of your mind generally. What is the course of its thoughts? How the mind reacts to any given situation, when the behaviour changes and in what situation, has to be observed. These are all more important aspects to any individual than the worldly entertainment they indulge in. Have you noticed most of the important waves of your mind have their roots to your childhood. Your transformation to a better human being depends mainly on self-observation, introspection, interrogation, analysing and cleansing.

We can make a complete chart of our life by analyzing our self. What are our merits and demerits? What are our beliefs and attitudes? What are our goals and achievements? What was our success and failure? There are three different pictures of any person. What actually he is, what actually he wants to be, what people view him as. It is better to make all the three as one.

List all your negative qualities and your positive traits. What do you want to actually achieve in this life? It's better to have a goal. Without goals, there is no purpose in life. Have a goal and have a commitment towards that goal. If you have a sincere commitment towards your high and positive goal, there is no need to talk of self-control or stability of mind. Your goal and commitment will bring everything to its place.

With your commitment towards your goal, you should bring continuous awareness of it every day, subconsciously in the process. Don't bring procrastination and postponement in between your goals. But do not take too big a goal. For example, if somebody is lame, can he think of mountaineering. Goals should be such that it is within your capacity and understanding. Dream high and think high. That itself will vanish all your negativities. Understand your own self and decide the purpose of your life and your goals.

After achieving your goals, it is very important to show gratitude towards nature. Before achieving the goals, it's important to visualize the goals. Prayers do help in achieving the goals, especially early mornings are the best time for praying and visualizing. Even if you have diverted from your path during your life journey, it never matters. You can always come back and start fresh. After all, life is a game. Do not take things so seriously that you end your life at the slightest provocation.

Your attitude towards life is more important. There are three kinds of people- the positive ones, who see positivity in everything, they are the optimists, the pessimists see the negative side of everything the neutral ones take life as it comes. Then there are people who live just to impress others. Whatever they do, it is based on what others will think of them. Some live independently with their own beliefs and opinions. Most of them are dictated by social norms and customs. Some want to be perfect in whatever they do. They are perfectionists, some are born critics, then there are gossip mongers who take great delight in discussing about others.

While achieving our goals one of the main obstacle may be fear. Once you overcome this fear, you can achieve success. Next obstacle may be doubt. Then there is impact of society on us, the rules and regulations laid down by them, which may be a hindrance in our development.

Especially women in India have undergone many such hurdles to achieve their goals for the past 50 years. There is a massive change in women in India. Majority of them have achieved their goals by driving this country to a better future. We have broken the shackles of many social evil like dowry, child marriage, sati, devadasi system. Every woman right from the rural level have become independent and are earning their own income, Nari Shakti or women energy is nothing but empowerment received by self-control and stability in mind. The more controlled and stable we are, we get more divine energy and willpower.

Do not make too many goals as it is difficult to concentrate. Having one goal at a time will bring focus. We should pay attention to the path, then the end will automatically be reached. Concentrate on the perfection to the process, then it will make you reach the end.

Chapter 4
Attachment and Detachment

*Photo taken by author

Many factors contribute to the imbalance of human mind and behavior. Being stable in all situations, even when provoked, is a great mastery of self. Though most of the emotions arise out of the accumulation of thoughts, among external factors, one aspect cannot be ignored, our attachment to our body, our family, our country, our caste, our religion, our friends, our belongings etcetera the list goes on.

Even though majority of us know that this world is not permanent and our relationships with people and things or temporary in nature, we find it very difficult to come out of the bonding with our dear ones. Our attachment is so deep that it is the basis of all our actions. This attachment cannot be ignored.

Then we have attachment to our body and its beauty. It's a truth that everyone loves his own self more than anything else. Don't we defend ourselves when accused or attacked by someone, don't we beautify ourselves even in old age. Is it not true that we love ourselves? Too much of love for our own self is only ego and vanity, devoid of which, we become down to earth. Even in our death bed, when we are in the threshold of death, our minds will still be wandering here and there for our dear ones.

Like in the previous chapter, we discussed about one truth that is death, which is universal. Here let us look at another truth that is, all things that you have, all people around you, all qualities or challenges that you possess are also temporary in nature. Nothing is going to stay with you till the end. Your own body is only a container of yourself. It will be destroyed the movement you die. Why then this attachment and detachment of worldly things and people? The great plan of the master that is nature is to come out victoriously from its play called Destiny.

There is a beautiful quote of Swami Vivekananda

"That man alone will be able to get the best of nature, who having the power of attaching himself to a thing with all his energy, has also the power to detach himself when he should do so."

Work with all your might with as much attachment as possible but should be able to detach when required. Attachment is the source of all pleasures. Same attachment is also source of our pain.

In true love and happiness give and don't expect anything. The more you give, the more you will receive from nature. Don't give for giving sake. But out of genuine love, unconditional love. A mother is the first example of true love. Right from the time of pregnancy, she nurtures the child in the womb with unconditional love. She keeps working for her whole family like a machine with no expectation. The love of Indian women is incomparable.

One way to Salvation in Hindu religion is through work or duty. That path is known as karma Yoga We should work with full might and perfection, but with the detached attitude, we should not get attached to the results of what we do. It can be success or failure. Never get depressed if it is failure or get carried away If it is success. Show your dedication to bring the perfection in the work and not to its results. That is, do with full concentration and selfless motive. At the same time, we should be in a position to detach ourselves when required.

Being selfless is your own expansion. The more selfless you are, the more you expand. Come out of closed doors and expand yourself in the universe. Make your love universal. Make your duty and responsibility universal. That is working with detached attitude.

Being selfish and self-centered only nurtures your emotions, feelings, and intentions on the negative side. Don't hit back for everything you face in life. To remain calm, composed and self-controlled even amidst turmoil requires super divine power. This attitude we call detached attitude.

Nothing can happen to us unless we make ourselves susceptible to it. This includes disease as well. We pave the way for whatever we are facing which no one is to be blamed. The root cause or the seed was first sown in our minds.

We always grumble and complain. We don't have control over our thoughts and our actions. If we can control our thoughts at the base level itself, many a mishap can be avoided. Always be conscious of the universal truth, then naturally your intentions, attitudes and actions will reflect accordingly. Whatever we possess is not permanent. In fact, we are not going to hold our body till the end of our life. Body is only a container in which we are placed. What then to speak of beauty, wealth, position, status, education, caste, religion, cadre, Etc.

Working with detached attitude doesn't mean not to have any love or compassion for your fellow beings. In fact, you must have genuine love for all beings, including animals, but without any Possessiveness, love everyone neutrally without any bias. Love your work, people and things but with a detached attitude. Love everyone for loves sake without selfishness irrespective of caste, religion, nation or any other division. Love is taking care, concern, compassion with tolerance and patience. Mother Teresa was a very good example of selfless love and compassion. Great leaders like Gandhi, Netaji and spiritual masters like Rama Krishna Paramahamsa and Swami Vivekananda had universal love of their fellow beings.

When you have attachment to the person you love, you will have expectations combined with possessiveness. Expectations lead to misery, which in turn leads to possessiveness and jealousy. If you are selfless, you will not expect anything. Too much of expectations and dreams only get you carried away. When you face failure, it leads to misery. This is a very important point to be noted.

The misery is so intense that many have even committed murders and suicides. Even small kids aged 10 years or 12 years commit suicide as they are unable to face failure. Just face life as it comes. Keep going on life's journey as it moves to green pastures and beautiful gardens at some places and to dark woods, face everything with a detached attitude and without any expectation.

Our attachment to our kith and kin and our wealth and possessions brings lot of pain and the desire to procure it brings more sorrow.

Always keep in your subconscious that this world is not permanent. Our stay here is only temporary. There is no need to overact for anything. Keep welcoming everything that happens to you. But act with intelligence in a calm and self-controlled manner.

Being a human being, it is but natural for anybody to get attracted to various excitements, beauties and entertainments which are surrounding us. At least majority of us know about the universal truth given in the above paragraphs. It is not that easy to come out of the clutches of this worldly. Drama. (known as Maya in Hindu religion)

With increase in money flow and attractions, expectations have increased.

While chasing your dreams and even while you are caught in the wheel of Maya, don't forget the universal truth, of the world being the stage and you the player and death the leveler. Getting yourself entangled in too much of expectations, in dreams, only lands in further misery and tragedy.

Chapter 5
Input Influences Thought

The concept of karma is as old as mankind. Karma comes as input even before we enter the womb, our original home. It is we who decide our mother even before we are born, these inputs continue till death and even after that. Many of your present karmas are the continuation of your previous births. Even people whom you meet in this birth and some important incidents or continuation of your previous births.

We get entangled with other beings in each life time causing further karmas with all of them. Mankind is like a toy in the hands of destiny. One may be good or rich or well educated or beautiful all due to destiny. Suffering in the hands of poverty, crime, Famine, etc. on one side while there is beauty and richness on the other side. It's all the game of Destiny. So we must have compassion for those who are helpless as criminals and for the downtrodden. Having compassion for even a criminal is a very high and noble thought. Hate the sin and not the sinner.

Love your fellow beings who are immersed in poverty and ignorance. Along with compassion don't forget to show gratitude to destiny for the good things in life.

Human beings are such wonderful creatures. You are not less than any God. Wonders have happened on this earth, no doubt. More than your body, your mind is so powerful that it has brought revolutions and innovations on this earth.

What input you give to yourself throughout your life is very important. That doesn't mean that you should always be away from evil and be surrounded by good. Like in health in thought also, you should be an immune person. Immune to face everything. Let us not be influenced by anything.

We face lots and lots of calamities external to our body and even more deeper and intense are the dangers which we face from within. Living a perfect life is better in saying than in doing.

When we talk of inputs, special mention of media has to be done. Media in the form of TV, mobile with all its attractions especially YouTube, Facebook, WhatsApp, Twitter and Instagram has made everyone addictive. This includes even the previous generation and senior citizens as well. Now a day this is the major input for all beings. People have forgotten or even feel lazy to read a book. Fifty years ago book was the major companion to the educated mass.

Of course there is better side to media which is more informative and makes people more smart and knowledgeable. With Google and internet, you get the knowledge and information on any subject. You can know the routes of new places. You can learn things online sitting at home. Mobile has brought the whole world in a nutshell. Communication and knowledge has increased. More and more people have become self-expressive. Media has given more freedom of expression and creativity.

Today's youth you are just few steps behind. To master yourself, it all depends on your next step. Which side are you going to turn? The right leads to positivity and the left to negativity. Use your own brain to choose the correct path. Make a strong goal in your life and practice your life in reaching that positive goal. To become well educated, rich or famous is not what I mean to see life in the right perspective, to analyse people and situations, especially politics and to be scientific in our approach and in our thoughts. Free from any bias of caste, religion, region or even language. Don't become a prey to any political leader based on religion or caste. Analyze yourself, you are your own leader.

As human beings, all are equal and are made of same blood and flesh. Respect everyone and see divinity in all beings irrespective of their character, status, religion or even past. Pay much attention to your inner self. And in developing a charismatic personality.

If history brought so many revolutions with limited resources, how much change can youth of today bring. There is so much of technology and innovation to bring the required dynamism. The whole world is in your hands. It's like building a temple. Each culture has its own contribution. Each individual can contribute to the betterment of society or nation.

The healthier the mind, the healthier is the body. Of course there could be other reasons for the body getting affected. Even if the body gets affected due to irregular eating patterns, due to bad habits or pollutions from outside, if the Willpower and internal courage and strength is mighty, you can understand the storm from outside, and you can courageously face it.

Very often the storm or even tsunami is from inside itself. Our mind, body and the senses are always in struggle with the internal and external world. When I say internal struggle, it means not only the mind. This struggle is voluntary. It also means the struggle of the internal organs due to our external Habits. This is involuntary and not known to us. However, the will power of the mind can greatly influence the body. Also, during Corona many survived more out of willpower than by medication. When we talk of health, food cannot be ignored. Intake of proper food not only gives us good health but also good mental wellbeing.

Every man cannot become God or everyman cannot become a demon.

We are all ordinary souls slowly travelling in the life's journey. Our preparation should begin from childhood itself, supported by parents and teachers. It is good to be trained by parental ideas and doctrines, but after certain stage it is better we grow independently. Freedom only gives growth, to explore new ideas and to express ourselves creatively and with innovation. Childhood is the best part of any human being's life. The inputs given during childhood are laid as foundation stone for the entire life. A child tumbles one stone upon another and with his own experience becomes a self-made man. Children of these days are like kites. Flying in the sky, tossed about and flying aimlessly. They hate to be advised, to be dictated and criticized. They become aggressive and arrogant. Honestly speaking, criticism brings the best in us. It is always good to live amidst people who criticize us than with people who praise us. Criticism is like eye opener when taken in the right sense.

Have you ever noticed the more you say no to a child it is more attracted to it? Even as adults, if anything is restricted or prohibited, we are more curious to know about it. We are more attracted to it. This is one of the reasons for increase in drugs, alcoholism, Prostitution, smuggling, adultery and other crimes as well.

Too much of control over a certain thing only makes it more attractive. To avoid such a situation, first of all self or children should be educated upon the consequences they will face while indulging in prohibited habits. Secondly, they have to be directed and habituated to a better habit. Sports, music, reading, dancing, swimming, etc. keeps the mind and body healthy. Fine Arts and sports, gardening, reading and writing enhances the personality of any individual.

*Photo taken by author

Chapter 6
Meditation

*Photo taken by author.

Meditation is a very ancient technique. It is a process by which all the stored up thoughts get cleansed and removed. Many feel that meditation is not for them as they cannot sit for too long and control their thought. It is good that you get more thoughts. Just like when we clean a dirty room, lot of dust comes out, similarly in meditation all the stored up thoughts come out. In fact, it is very good to practice meditation as a routine. I would recommend everyone to practice meditation twice a day. It is cleansing for the mind.

Initially all negative emotions will come out. Emotions like anger, lust, desire, greed, fear, impulsiveness will come out. If you are persistent in your practice and continuously aware of your goals and universal truth,gradually you will become a calm person.

Before getting initiated into any mantra for at least few months sit in a calm place and just allow the mind to run, you just be the witness and observe it. When the mind comes to know that it is being observed, gradually thoughts reduce. Same thing can be followed with our actions. We can continuously keep a watch on our day to day actions and emotions by diarising and giving marks to ourselves. Marks is for self-motivation and tracking the thought and behaviour process. Though we may not get success immediately, as years go by, we will transform into a self-controlled and stable person. It may take a whole lifetime also depending upon the karma stored in our consciousness.

As you allow your mind to run, you observe your breath. The incoming. and outgoing of your breath. This is your life force. Once this stops, your life is over. One step further with closed eyes you can concentrate on the space in between your eyebrows. By doing the above three steps your thoughts and emotions get regulated, though it might get turbulent in the beginning.

There are various other kinds of meditation which can be learnt from Gurus. Chanting of mantras cools the mind throughout the day. Specially chanting of OM loudly at least for 15 minutes gives balance to the body and mind. Many a bad habit can be eradicated by daily chanting of OM.

It will all sound quite absurd for people of this age. But most of them are in confusion and dilemma, living without a purpose. When they come across a small failure or insult they go to extreme ends of killing others or ending their own life. They are not balanced in their emotions and behavior.

Along with meditation and chanting, if you add pranayama and yoga to your life, it will bring out the beautiful self in you. The intention of each being is to be peaceful and happy. Let us be peaceful when the route is as clear as that, to have a regulated thought process. What can be a better exercise than meditation? Meditation done during the early hours of dawn is more fruitful.

According to Patanjali,A great yogic. Master of ancient times. Meditation can be divided into 3. First part is bringing the mind from wavering thoughts to a concentrated point. Which is called as dharna. The second part is actually meditation, dhyana. The final part is Samadhi which normally only saints and spiritual leaders attain. In this stage the individual consciousness becomes one with the universal consciousness.

A hollow canal runs through your spine. The left nerve is Eda and the right nerve Pingala. The hollow canal is known as Sushumna. There are 7 chakras starting from the base of the spine to the crown of the head. As we progress in meditation, our mind passes through all these chakras. Upon reaching the crown of the head, Samadhi is attained.

Further the mind can be purified by pranayama. Doing pranayama Just before meditation only enhances the process. The procedure goes like this. First, the body has to be regulated with yoga and exercises. Next, the breath has to be regulated with pranayama or breathing exercises. Then the mind can be regulated with chanting of Om before entering into meditation. All this when done between 4 to 6:00 in the morning gives better results. Early dawn is known as Brahma Muhurta. At this time, we get divine energy from the universal consciousness. There are variety of pranayama techniques which can be learnt from a proper Guru.

Later during the day also, we have to be consciously aware of our own self, observing, analysing our moves. All this will help us not to become a victim of worldly attractions or Maya. By these processes criminal activities like bribery, adulteration, addictions divorce Etc. can be reduced if not eliminated.

Every human being who has come to this world has a responsibility of conducting himself in the best possible way so as to not to disturb the equilibrium of the universe. I know to err is human, to forgive is divine. All humans are prone to make mistakes. By mistakes only we learn our lessons. With each experience, we have to grow and develop and not become gloomy and depressed.

Chapter 7
Universal Mass

Love is the greatest expression of divinity. We Love because we are divine. We are all part of one Universal mass's discussed earlier, Love is, not expecting anything in return. It's not barter system. Our parents are best examples of divine love. especially the mother, she is the epitome of sacrifice and love.

To be selfless and caring for the other person is Love.

When we come out of our individual self, to move to the next person, it is Love. We can expand our self to the family, our street, our town, our country, and the whole universe until our love becomes universal in nature.

To see God in all beings, In all creatures even animals, insects, in snakes and tigers. To see divinity everywhere and in everything we do is the doctrine of Hindu religion. Literally start seeing God in all beings at least for one day of your life. You will know the tremendous difference it creates.

All negative qualities vanish with this kind of attitude. You become a fountain of gratitude, generosity, Sacrifice, passionate to help the poor and the downtrodden. All base desires like greed and lust vanishes. You go beyond the physical appearance of the person or creature. When you see the inner divinity, you become fearless and compassionate to become a being of tolerance and patience.

This universal Love will make you universally responsible. There are so many injustices happening around you. Is it not the responsibility of modern youth to eliminate the crimes? Should you be the drug addict or the Messiah clearing drug menace? Should you be the drunkard or the Messiah clearing the menace, you should be the torch bearer. Every human being has a purpose to live here, the moment you realize this you have become universally responsible.

Forget yourself, your own comforts. Think of others and help others. The more passionate you are in helping others, the more divine love flows in. Another greatest help that all individuals can do is to think positively and with gratitude. Positive thoughts give us strength and negative thoughts leads us to weakness.

As humans we are leaving our thoughts as footprints for posterity and for our own karma. Accept life as it comes without any reaction. Do not put your nose into what the other person is doing., it is his Karma and he knows how to tackle it. You can help him but not pinpoint at him. To each his own Will and Karma, love your neighbour as how you love yourself.

In marriages, If the partners become selfless and live for the sake of the other person by seeing divinity in them, number of divorces can be reduced. What you give, you get back. This holds good not only among couples, but in all relationships. We should accept all relations as they are. We should stand in their shoes to know their point of view.

There is so much of hatred and crime spreading everywhere. People are ill-treated in the name of caste and religion. Human beings have forgotten their original divinity. Divinity lies not in temples and statues. The actual

God is within all creatures. Showing love and respect to mankind and gods other creations is true devotion.

Due to such biased behavior from society, the downtrodden and their children are facing so many problems. Due to difference in opinion among religions, in their own country, many are deprived of their freedom of expression, social development and financial development. Due to all this

innocent youngsters become victims of Naxalites and terrorism, very often they themselves become terrorists. It is a duty of all political and national leaders to pave way for a better society where everyone can live in harmony and security.

But wherever there is injustice, people have to stand in unity and fight for it. To keep quiet or grumble is not the solution. Failure is only stepping stone to success. We should take each insult; each blow as a stepping stone to move further. We should hit back with all our might; this is one of the first lessons in the Bhagwat Gita to fight for justice. Fighting for a true cause is good karma. The downtrodden and the victims of injustice should not sit with the doors closed. Come out in the bright light and fight for your cause. You are not a sheep You are a brave lion.

Even though women are Emancipated and empowered on one side, still women are facing lot of insults and violence in society. So much of agony they face doing multi tasks and facing challenges everywhere. Eve teasing and rapes are on the rise.

Due to all this more and more women are undergoing depression and other psychological trauma. Of late such heinous crimes have happened to women in the name of religion and caste. It is the universal responsibility of others to come out and fight for their causes.

Too much of negative karma is spreading in the universal mass. In the long run this will affect the karma of all beings. Very recently we saw huge sweep of Corona which existed for nearly 4 to 5 years. Economy of all the nations were affected. We lost so many lives.

To quote a beautiful poem by Swami Vivekananda.

Requiescat. In pace.

Speed forth O Soul! Upon thy star strewn path;

Speed blissful one! Where thought is ever free,

where time and space is no longer mist the view,

Eternal peace and blessings be with thee!

Thy service true, complete thy sacrifice,

Thy home the heart of love transcendent find;

Remembrance sweet, that kills all space and time,

Like altar roses fill thy place behind.!

Thy bonds are breaking, thy quest in bliss is found;

And one with that which comes as death and life;

Thou helpful one! unselfish ever on earth

Ahead! still help with love this world of strife!

The real divinity of man cannot be understood and measured. It has been a mystery since ancient times. What is soul how it passes from one birth to another birth.

All those who are suffering and victimized both by destiny and people, kindly listen to this poem written below by Swami Vivekananda. There is still hope, Don't lose your heart.

"Hold on yet a while, Braveheart."

If the sun by the cloud is hidden a bit,

If the welkin shows but gloom,

Still hold on yet a while, brave heart,

The victory is sure to come.

No winter was but summer came behind,

Each hollow crests the wave,

They push each other in light and shade;

Be steady then and brave.

The duties of life are sore indeed,

And its pleasures fleeting vain,

The goal so shadowy seems and din,

Yet plod on through the dark, brave heart,

With all thy might and main.

Not a work will be lost, no struggle vain,

Though hopes be blighted, powers gone;

Of thy loins shall come the heirs to all,

Then hold on year a while brave soul,

No good is ever undone

Though the good and the wise in life are few,

Yet theirs are the reins to lead,

The masses know but late the worth;

Heed none and gently guide.

With thee are those who see afar,

With thee are the Lord of might,

All blessings pour on the great soul

To thee may all come right!

We are all ordinary mortals. Internally like a sapling yet to grow. It is not possible for everyone to reach the grandeur, as quoted by Swami Vivekananda" I'm in everything in everybody. I am in all lives I am the universe. "Nor can everyone pursue the infinite and the struggle to grasp the infinite. As ordinary human beings, we can strive for a pure and moral life which will lead to perfection. It's enough if as ordinary mortals we remember that God or universal power is our own self. God is in all creatures only we are too ignorant to know the truth. We are caught by Maya. Maya is nothing but our own desires and temptations. The moment you bring divinity into everyone you see, and in everything you do, Maya and its clutches gets defeated. Our original nature is divinity. We are all divine beings. To discover divinity from within is actual concept and purpose of life, we may fail several times. It may take several lifetimes also, do not be defeated. Keep striving and climbing to reach your peak of divinity.

Most of our energy is utilized in preserving our body, our family and partly in influencing others and getting influenced by them. Nowadays more than half a time is devoted to entertainment and enjoyment.

Yoga, Pranayama, meditation helps in developing the inner personality of men. The man who can control himself, can control others as well, as all minds are made of same material. To quote Swami

"This mind is a part of the Universal mind. Each mind is connected with every other mind, and each mind, wherever it is located, is in actual communication with the whole world. Mind is universal."

One secret to be learnt in life is- that soul is an awakened one who works and loves to the fullest extent, yet they are detached from everything. We are caught and sorrowful because we expect too much from others. We barter with our emotions and feelings. We expect too much from life. Give and don't expect anything back. Don't feel sad to give. Give happily to everyone without bargaining. Be selfless and keep giving. Only then you will receive more from nature.

There is no misery undeserved. We paved the way for everything. One who escapes misery and sorrow also escapes pleasure. If thought pattern is a tree, character is the main trunk which branches out as behaviour, habits, manners, attitudes, beliefs and opinions moulds. Our thought pattern, which grew along with the body over the years, mainly depends upon the beliefs and opinions. Beliefs and opinions molds the attitude which in turn brings out the behaviour, habits and manners. As told earlier our Destiny ultimately depends upon the store of thoughts in our mind. To repeat, do not be too proud of yourself or too sorrowful of your ill fate. Do not be critical or too controversial of anything just because you are not aware or have any knowledge of that subject. There is a saying by Christ. "Judge not that ye be not judged."

To quote Swami.

"The Man whom I am criticizing as not good maybe wonderfully so in some points in which I am not"

Whomever we love, in the background, each one of us project our own ideal and we are working on it.

Let us not complicate with too many ideas and beliefs. Life is as simple as that. Just face everything with a detached and self-controlled manner. Be stable in all situations. Let us be universally loving and responsible. For that we have to see the divine power in everyone and in everything. We are neither the body nor the mind. We are All Souls, part of one huge Universal mass or power. Let us live with purified thought and behavior. Loving our fellow beings is only universal religion. After all life is temporary why fight for petty issues. We come empty handed and we leave our body without any possession. Why then to complicate our life here, which is short and temporary. Let us spread the fragrance of love and unity.

ODE TO MY FRIEND

Fragrance of thy love

Has been blowing like a breeze

Time and distance

were never a hindrance

We selected each other

Among the millions

Are you the gift of God to me?

Thou art who

To whom I am destined to follow

From previous birth to next

You stood like a rock

Beating and bearing the storms

This is an ode to you

A small gift to you

My dear friend

Chapter 8
My Personal Experience and My Spiritual Journey

*Photo of author at the age of 4

I was born on 23rd April. 1963. In a small town called Vellore, In Tamil Nadu. My grandfather, J. Rama Swami, was a spiritual seeker who taught us how to live without hurting anyone. He did service to the poor and the downtrodden and literally taught us what it is to see divinity in man. He practiced yoga and meditation every day of his life. He was an honest and hardworking gentleman. Unfortunately, he expired when I was a 5-year-old girl. Just one month before his death I met him in my home town, while parting from him, even as a little girl, something made me cry bitterly saying "I will not part from you, my grandpa." Though he is no more with us, his genes and the knowledge he gained from his gurus have been transmitted to me. As a little girl I was always full of creativity and imagination. My father was in the Army. So we were shifted several times. Best part of my childhood was spent in Avadi with my friends Lakshmi, Suman, Ramesh, Manjula, Parveen, Uma and many others.

I studied in KVHVF till the age of 13 before getting shifted to Bhuj.

There were wonderful teachers who taught us excellently. Sanskrit was our 3rd language. 20 stanzas from Bhagwat Gita greatly impressed me. I kept repeating it loudly. Lord Krishna became my favorite God. I wanted to live my life according to the Gita. At the age of 21, I got a job as a probationary officer in Andhra Bank. But my mind always had a spiritual quest for God and to follow Bhagwat Gita. Those days in 1986, there were not many spiritual gurus as of now. I wanted to practice meditation every day. Each time I sat in meditation, there was a heavy rush of thoughts, and a lot of noise pollution. I felt very desperate.

As a Probationary Officer I felt very happy that I could break the orthodox chains of my father.

I felt independent and definitely it was an achievement for me to stand on my own legs at the age of 21. Those days' women were not given freedom, hardly 10% of the women went for a job. During such a time, I felt proud to travel alone from Bombay to Chennai and back, to live all alone independently facing new challenges as an officer.

The sub manager of the branch was a very harsh person, who reprimanded me for everything. I had a tough time far away from home, living and working amidst strangers. Some of them even tried to chase me away from my job.

My second place of posting after 6 months was Malakpet, Hyderabad. Though the colleagues were quite normal, I had horrible or rather terrible experiences at home. I lived as a paying guest in a house where only one old lady and her granddaughter lived. A separate room with a cot and dressing table was given. It was here that I got some strange experiences. Whenever the clock struck 12 every night a bunch of hair used to fly just above me and I was so terrified. In order to avoid those scenes, I started sleeping late at 2:00 or 3:00 AM. Suddenly, for one week they left me alone in the house. I bravely faced the whole week. One fine day while cleaning their house, I found a huge bunch of long hair in one box. When the owner of the house returned, I inquired them about the hair and told her about the nightmares I was facing every night. To my surprise and shock they told me that the girl's mother committed suicide by burning herself and she died on the very same bed in which I was sleeping every day. That long hair also belonged to the same woman. Anyway, my posting at the place was coming to an end and I left the place happily to my parents' house in Chennai. Meanwhile I got married and after one year I had to revisit Hyderabad to write my confirmation test. But the greatest shock was that the ghost returned at 12:00. O'clock. I had not even closed my eyes, but I could see a woman with long hair sitting next to me. I shrieked out of fear.

But my behaviour changed a lot after this incident. I felt lonely and there were frequent outbursts of various emotions. Life changed completely after marriage. It was a complete new atmosphere, with relatives who were not that supportive during those days. Unable to cope up at the domestic front and with lot of pressure in the office, I felt myself lost in a busy world with no friend to call my own. I was suffering from premenstrual tension which is caused due to hormonal changes. My infant was too small and he underwent 2 operations which made me more depressed. I felt I was not fit for marriage and this hustle bustle of life. I wanted to join the missionaries of Charity run by Mother Teresa to serve the poor.

I tried to run away to Calcutta, but destiny was kind enough that it made me miss the train at the last moment.

It was then that I decided to face life as it comes from a new angle. To face everything bravely, not to run away from it. My special gratitude to my friends in Mylapore branch who introduced me to Ramakrishna Mutt and books of Swami Vivekananda. My frequent visits to the Mutt and by reading the great volumes of Swami-ji, I could transform my life to a new leaf. I got proper initiation into Transcendental Meditation in 1989. At the time of initiation, I got a vision of a big hand blessing me. Lord Maha Vishnu appeared with Adi sesha. After these unique visions, I practiced my meditations seriously. In 1994, I learnt meditation from Swami Buteshanandji of Rama Krishna Math.I also read the life stories of Rama Krishna Paramahamsa and even took counselling from Swami Gautamananda. I used to feel so lonely during those days that I cried intensely one whole night, to get the vision of God and Lo I could see baby Krishna sitting next to me.

Gradually I started analyzing me by writing out my merits and demerits. I tried to live my life according to Gita. But too much of suppression only leads to the opposite. In my experiments with life I learnt a lot. In 1994 after my father's death I was transferred to a village called Pichatur. Here I got the opportunity to climb Tirumala hills, abode of Lord Venkateswara at least 9 times. Here again I got introduced to the great avatar shirdi sai baba. One day while climbing the tirumala mountains i wanted to test the existence of God.As I was alone I prayed to God to give me His vision. Surprisingly someone resembling Shirdi Baba was sitting on the steps giving me the required vision. I was too frightened to go near him.

I returned back from Pichatur in 1998 and I got the opportunity to learn many more meditations. On one side I was learning yoga and meditations and on the other side there were equally challenging problems to face. I always decided to be stable in whatever the situation may be. Of course there were some supportive colleagues who helped me a lot.

There is one more incident which is difficult to believe. On one fine Saturday afternoon I was returning back from my office to the bus stand in a place called Maduravoyal in Chennai. One big ox was tied to a nearby post. Absent mindedly I walked near the ox and very soon found myself being lifted in a fraction of second. I found the horns of the ox near my stomach. Somehow I gathered courage and pushed the horns and fell on the ground with trembling legs. I started fleeing from the place with as much strength as possible. As the ox was tied it didn't chase me.

To this day I am firm in my stability of mind and self-control, though at times I get deviated and burst out with variety of emotions.

This book itself is a dedication to mankind to share my knowledge and experiences. Everything is in our hands though our life is dictated by destiny. Still we can successfully come out from any given situation provided we have strong will and belief in nature or the universal power. We have to surrender ourself to God and see divinity in everything and whatever we do. People may criticise and insult us, but our conscious knows that we are always on a spiritual path.

Chapter 9
Swami Vivekananda

This chapter is a special dedication to my spiritual master Swami Vivekananda. Now a days there is lot of hustle bustle in the name of religion and spirituality. People have commercialized education and religion. Religion is being used in promoting politics as well. The real nature sof Hinduism has taken a very bad shape. Now is the time to remind people of the great souls of Swami Vivekananda and Ramakrishna Paramahamsa. I am debted to these great souls for shaping my inner peace and tranquility.

Swami Vivekananda was born on January 12 1863 in Calcutta. He was. named as Narendranath Datta. He was born on Maha Sankranthi day to a pious mother, who was a great devotee of Lord Shiva. As a little boy, Narendra was always restless and energetic, that his mother found it difficult to control him. As a student, he showed great talents and intelligence along with his leadership qualities. Even as a little boy, he felt all humans were one. He was scientific and analytical in his approach. He never believed anything just because it was written in a book or was told by any great man. He confirmed only by testing it himself. He grew up to a young man interested in music, drama, sports and reading. He was a storehouse of knowledge well versed by his intellectual and vast reading.

During his childhood also, he showed signs of deep meditation. Infact at the age of 15, he experienced his first spiritual ecstasy.

His first meeting with Rama Krishna Paramahamsa was a turning point in his life. Unlike many others of his age, he was a boy of purity and chastity as taught by his mother. His pure and deeper self was always drawn to the life of renunciation. His spiritual master Sri Ramakrishna was very fond of him. It was an everlasting bond of love and devotion between the two. Young Narendras goal was to realize God and for this he took instructions and guidance from Shri Ramakrishna. Shri Ramakrishnas joy knew no bounds when he saw young Naren for the first time. It looked as if the former was looking for him for several years. Gradually Shri Ramakrishna trained young Narendra in such a way that during meditations the lad could feel his body separate from his soul. Though the external struggle in spirituality was by Naren, the actual inner transformation was done by his Master. Early in his life Naren lost his father and had a huge family with lot of debts to be paid. He suffered in acute poverty and was so depressed and even wondered if God really existed. It was during these times. On one rainy day, he got some spiritual experiences in which he felt all his questions of life were being answered, all the mysteries getting removed veil by veil.

After this revelation his attitude to life changed. He was convinced that his life was determined to become a monk and to serve the humanity. More than anything as human beings we need guidance from a true master. That great master was Sri Rama Krishna Paramahamsa who paved all his knowledge and spiritual training to his sincere devotee Naren who in later days became Swami Vivekananda.

Though basically young Naren did not believe in rituals and Pooja and in idol worship, Shri Ramakrishna gradually Initiated him in worshipping the universal mother. As Naren was in acute poverty, Sri Ramakrishna asked him to pray for his worldly benefits. But on nearing the Goddess each time his mind only prayed for spiritual upliftment. Young Narendra was always pure in thought and mind and he guided the other boys who were under Ramakrishna in the same way. He Insisted upon chastity, purity, self-control and renunciation. Shri Ramakrishna's teachings were revolved around Love for God and love and service for mankind by seeing divinity in all. Real spirituality as told by them over and over again was eradication of worldly tendencies and the development of Man's higher nature.

Shri Ramakrishna initiated several of the young disciples into the monastic life, making Naren the leader. And thus he himself founded the Rama Krishna order of monks.

Swamiji travelled as a wandering monk from the Himalayas to Kanyakumari. Sitting on a rock he felt deeply for the nation. He was a patriot and a prophet all in one. His heart writhed with pain looking at the common man's poverty and helplessness in the hands of the rich and the so called leaders. He wanted to bring the glory of our Nation to the external world. He attended the Parliament of Religions in Chicago representing Hinduism and India.

Further details of his service to Mankind will be highlighted in my upcoming books.

Let us end this book with a quote by Swamiji "True freedom and bliss could be attained only by the individual and not by the masses as a whole".

Chapter 10
Conclusion

With this I conclude this book. Wish you all a bright future.

Let us remember to have pure thoughts. As the individual mind is always in communion with the universal mind. Our thoughts definitely contribute to the mighty ocean of Universal Mind. To bring peace, harmony in society and to fill it with the love and happiness ultimately lies in our hands. We must consciously see divinity in everything and everyone. This is the highest sadhana. Practicing this itself will cleanse your attitudes, beliefs and opinions.

Remember we are neither the body nor the mind. We are all unseen souls permanent in nature. This is a body which gets destroyed in each birth. Our thoughts get carried forward in the form of karma, striving to live a stable and self-controlled life and by seeing divinity everywhere and in everyone. We are moving forward to universal truth. We may not be successful in our equilibrium in one lifetime. But our soul keeps moving to the next stage for a better being and to get merged with the universal nature. As we all know that nature is uniform everywhere, God or universal power is also one. For our convenience we have divided them into various names and religions. Let us all March towards one universal religion that is love. Divine love knows no bartering. Divine love is like a candle, illuminating others and serving others. Forgive yourself and expand your little self to include the whole universe. See divinity everywhere and in everything. Gradually you can feel the warmth of divine love.

See you all in a yet another project very soon.

Some of the Divine Souls of India